The Positive Power Workbook

Conny Jasper

Copyright © 2020 by Conny Jasper

All rights reserved. No part of this book may be reproduced in any form by any means without prior written permission of the author, except for brief quotations used in connection with a review.

ISBN 978-0-9889361-0-2

Published by:

Conny Jasper
PO Box 6442
Somerset, NJ 08875

Third printing: June 2020

The Positive Power Workbook

Positive power is the ability to empower yourself in a positive way. It is a way of thinking and acting that facilitates optimistic and constructive energy in your life. Positive power helps to generate incentive and transformation. By using positive power, you can take a challenging situation and make it a creative one. You can turn it into an empowering opportunity. This is done through the use of affirmations and mental energy.

Affirmations involve consciously thinking or speaking a group of words or sentences that are intended to create positive results. These statements are used to persuade both your unconscious and conscious mind. Your mind is a system that is programmed by both external and internal influences. Empowerment happens when you take control of how you program your psyche. To *affirm* means *to strengthen.*

Affirmations are motivational. They are designed to give you the incentive to better yourself and your life. The more specific you are with an affirmation the better it will work. Your mind understands very direct and clear instructions. Also, the more often it is repeated the more effective it will be. Repetition can be a useful device. The more frequently you repeat something the more likely it will be put into practice. Affirmations are like prayers or incantations. Words can be very powerful.

This workbook will help you to think about many important aspects of your life. It is organized into three areas: Personal Power, Money Power, and Love Power. The Personal Power section concerns diverse aspects of personal empowerment. Money Power relates to money, investments, and career. And the Love Power section involves emotions and relationships. Take the time to read through the various affirmational statements in each section. Because of similarity, some affirmations are grouped together. They are all accompanied by a brief commentary and one or more questions. Examine each of the questions, and answer them thoughtfully. Do not be concerned with the exact meaning of the question. Only answer it the way that you interpret it. This workbook allows for your own self-discovery and personal decision making. You can use a notebook or a pad to write down your answers to the questions.

Then the next step is to put the effort into what you have learned, and use this book as a tool for action. Make it happen. Create your life the way that you want to. And remember that you can produce your own reality, but you are also dealing with everyone else's reality. That means we live in a world where others are also creating various circumstances with their thoughts and actions.

As an aid to your efforts, you can write an affirmation on a sticky note and put it in a place where you will see it often. You can also use index cards that you can carry with you wherever you go. Or you can put them in a deck to shuffle and choose a daily card.

~ Personal Power ~

1. "I am grounded and connected in my body."

   Being grounded and connected means being stable and balanced. This is the most important part of developing and maintaining empowerment. It is challenging to be 100 percent grounded at all times. That is why it is necessary to continually remind yourself to ground and connect.

~ How do you feel about your body?

~ How do you stay in tune with your body?

~ How do you get grounded within your physical self?

~ What helps you to feel connected with your body?

2. "I am grounded and connected with the earth."

   When you are grounded and connected with the earth, you are in touch with the natural world. You are aware of who and what is around you. You are aware of the sights, sounds, and smells that are around you. And you are aware of changes in the weather and changes in the seasons. Being grounded and connected with the earth also means spending time with the natural world.

~ How do you stay in tune with the natural world?

~ How do you get grounded with the earth?

~ What helps you to feel connected with the earth?

3. "I am fully present in my body."

   Your body is the container of your consciousness. Being present in your body means being available to yourself. Physical presence means being aware of yourself as a physical organism. It is an aspect of wholeness.

~ How do you stay present in your body?

~ How do you maintain physical consciousness?

4. "I am fully present in the world."

   When you are present in the world, you are living with awareness. You are able to connect with the world around you. You are able to stay in the moment. You are in the world in a healthy way.

~ How do you relate to the world around you?

~ How do you remain present in the moment?

~ How do you create a healthy connection with your environment?

5. "My body is sacred."

   Your body is the vessel of all your emotional, mental, physical, and spiritual processes. When you honor your body and your self, you help to create health and wholeness within yourself and around yourself.

~ What does sacredness mean to you?

~ How do you honor your physical self?

6. "I feel comfortable in my body."

Feeling comfortable in your body is necessary for physical and mental health. This does not mean that you will never feel uncomfortable. We all experience illness or pain from time to time. Feeling comfortable in your body means accepting all of your physical functions and needs. And it means taking care of all your physical functions and needs in a way that produces the best possible state of well-being.

~ Are you able to accept that you are a physical being with all kinds of different physical functions?

~ How do you feel about your body and your physical functions?

~ In what ways do you create quality of life for yourself?

7. "I take care of my body and my health."

Caring for your body and your health creates stability and well-being. There is a saying that goes, "health equals wealth." Health is also essential to empowerment.

~ How do you take care of your body?

~ How do you take care of your health?

8. "I take good care of myself, and I know how to heal myself."

Taking care of yourself is more than taking care of your body. It is also necessary to take care of you mind, emotions, and spirit. This helps to create wholeness. In a world filled with so much stress and complications, healing is an ongoing process.

~ How do you take care of yourself overall?

~ What do you do to heal yourself on a regular basis?

9. "I am able to heal myself when I am feeling stressed and tense."

Modern society is filled with complexities and stresses. This makes it necessary for us to have a constant awareness of the energies that effect us. It also makes it necessary to continually heal the tension so that it does not build up in the body and the mind.

~ Do you know when you are feeling stressed and tense?

~ What do you do to relieve the pressure?

10. "I exercise regularly and keep myself physically fit."

Moving your body, and using your muscles, is necessary for physical and mental health. It is beneficial to blood circulation, heart movement, and respiration. It also helps to keep your bones strong. In addition, exercise releases endorphins, which are natural tranquilizing and pain-relieving chemicals in the body.

~ What kinds of physical exercises do you practice?

~ Do you have a regular fitness program?

11. "I consistently replenish myself."

There are many ways to replenish yourself. Replenishment can happen physically, mentally, emotionally, and spiritually. Your body, mind, and soul are a system through which various kinds of energies continually flow.

~ What does replenishment mean to you?

~ How do you replenish yourself?

12. "I am nourished by the powers of Nature."

Nature is the source of life. We are born from Nature, sustained by Nature, and then returned to Nature. It is an important part of health and well-being to stay connected with and supported by Nature.

~ In what ways are you nourished by Nature?

13. "I remember to breathe fully and deeply."

Proper breathing is another important aspect of physical and mental health. Breathing is something that we do on a continual basis. Stress causes short and shallow breathing. Therefore, it is important to be aware of the breath, and remember to breathe properly.

~ Are you consistently aware of your breathing?

~ Do you allow yourself to breathe fully and deeply?

14. "I get plenty of clean, fresh air."

Clean, fresh air is necessary for good health. Our lungs continually need air. We are sustained by a constant flow of inhalation and exhalation.

~ Do you open the windows on a nice day?

~ Do you spend time sitting or walking outdoors?

~ Do you minimize your exposure to polluted air?

15. "I expose myself to a healthy amount of light."

	In modern times, we spend a lot of hours indoors. That means that we are exposed to a lot of unnatural lighting. Many of us get very little light exposure. It is a known fact that a lack of exposure to light can cause depression. Too little light can also cause drowsiness. A healthy amount of light exposure creates health and well-being.

~ Do you get enough light exposure?

16. "I regularly replenish my body with fresh, clean water."

	Water is cleansing and refreshing. Good health requires a regular intake of water. Our bodies are made of about 70% water. So it is necessary to keep your body hydrated.

~ How much water do you drink on a daily basis?

17. "I have a positive and healthy relationship with food."

	Food is one of the things that sustains you. It is a source of nourishment and energy. Healthy food provides sustenance for all your organs and bodily functions.

~ What kinds of foods do you eat?

~ Do you take the time to prepare healthy meals?

~ Do you enjoy your meals?

18. "I take the time to learn about proper diet and nutrition."

A healthy diet with proper nutrition is what powers us and gives us energy. One of the ways that we take in positive energy is through positive food sources. In modern times there is a lot of hype and misinformation about food. Therefore, it is necessary to learn about what your body really needs to stay healthy.

~ Do you seek information about diet and nutrition?

~ How much do you know about vitamins, minerals, and protein?

~ Are you getting a sufficient amount of all the nutrients that your body needs?

~ Do you vary the kinds of foods that you eat?

19. "I use my energy in healthy and balanced ways."

Your body has only a certain amount of energy to use in a given period of time. You need periods of activity and periods of rest. Empowerment is knowing how and when to use your energy.

~ Do you maintain an awareness of your energy level?

~ How do you balance the use of your energy?

~ Are you productive with the energy that you have?

20. "I create stability within myself and in my environment."
21. "I am stable and well grounded."

Stability is strength. To establish stability both within yourself and outside of yourself is to establish a balance in your life. It is the foundation of empowerment.

~ Do you pay attention to what you are doing?

~ How do you create stability within yourself?

~ How do you create stability in your environment?

22. "I give myself support and comfort."

Giving yourself support and comfort means acknowledging what your needs are and taking care of them. It is also about soothing yourself when you are tired, tense, ill, or emotionally distraught.

~ How do you give yourself support?

~ How do you give yourself comfort?

23. "I give myself time for relaxation and recreation."

Relaxation and recreation are important ways to relieve stress. Besides working and accomplishing our goals, we need to have time for fun. And we need time for rest.

~ What do you do for enjoyment?

~ What do you do for relaxation?

24. "I am able to relax and let go."

Too much stress can cause physical and emotional problems. So it is necessary to know when to let go and unwind. There are many ways to relax and relieve stress. Getting enough restful sleep is one of the most essential ways.

~ How do you relax and let go?
~ What do you do to relieve stress?

~ Do you get enough sleep on a regular basis?

25. "I take care of my emotional well-being."

During the busy activities of life, it is important to maintain awareness of your emotions. Blocking or suppressing your feelings creates an imbalance. It is healthy to acknowledge what you are feeling and to process your emotions.

~ Do you pay attention to your emotions?

~ How do you take care of your emotional well-being?

26. "I know how to ask for assistance from others."

Part of taking care of yourself is knowing when to ask for help with something. Independence is a good thing, but so is interdependence. Nobody will know that you need or want something unless you ask for it.

~ Are you able to ask for assistance when you need it?

~ Are you appreciative when someone helps you?

27. "I have a healthy sense of humor."

Humor is a great way to ease tension. Laughter is a natural mood elevator. And comedy is an excellent source of entertainment. It helps to alleviate life's challenges and difficulties. And it helps to make life more enjoyable.

~ What provides amusement for you?

~ How do you express your sense of humor?

28. "My home is a safe and comfortable place."

Your home is where you sleep, eat, relax, keep your belongings, and entertain company. It is necessary for well-being to feel secure in your home. Home should be a sanctuary.

~ Do you live in a place where you are comfortable?

~ Do you live in a place where you feel safe?

29. "I am centered in my body, mind, emotions, and spirit."

Centering is similar to grounding and connecting. When you are centered, you are balanced and clear. Centering means bringing yourself into alignment.

~ What makes you feel centered?

~ How do you bring yourself back to center when you are feeling un-centered?

30. "I work to maintain a balance between my spiritual needs and my material needs."

The pursuit of happiness is much more than the pursuit of material goods. Material goods can provide physical comfort, but spirituality can provide mental and emotional balance.

~ How do you balance your material needs with your spiritual needs?

31. "I have a healthy sense of self confidence."

Having self confidence means that you believe in yourself. It means that you have personal security. When you have confidence in yourself, you do not let negative people or situations stand in your way. You are able to proceed with assurance in your abilities.

~ What do you do to build and maintain confidence in yourself?

32. "I seek to empower myself in healthy and balanced ways."

To empower yourself is to give yourself inner strength and embody competence. In today's world, it is important to discover ways to empower yourself. Healthy empowerment is power with, rather than power over. It means that you manage yourself with strength and integrity, not in a way that is manipulative or controlling.

~ What makes you feel empowered?

~ How do you consistently empower yourself?

33. "I have realistic goals for my future."

It is important to have goals, but it is equally important to have realistic goals. Too much time and money can be wasted on impractical ambitions. When pursuing something, it is necessary to understand everything that is involved in the process.

~ What is important to you?

~ What do you really want?

~ Is it a plausible goal?

~ What is or would be the first step that you would need to take in order to make it happen?

34. "I am accomplishing my goals with great success."

Accomplishing your goals means being able to make a commitment. It also requires that you be patient during the time that it takes to bring your goals to fruition.

~ What are the steps that you are taking, or that you need to take, in order to accomplish your goals?

~ What are all of your major goals?

~ What are all of your minor goals?

~ Are you aware of all your major and minor successes?

35. "I am comfortable with success."

Part of being successful is the ability to be comfortable with it. Success can be scary, because it involves responsibility. When you are successful, you accumulate obligations. So you need to be comfortable with that.

~ What does success mean to you?

~ How do you feel about success?

36. "I am able to make practical decisions."

Every day we make both minor and major decisions. Making choices is a regular part of life. While you cannot know everything that there is to know, clear-headed decisions usually give you the best results.

~ What helps you to make sensible decisions?

37. "I know what my priorities are, and I take care of them first."

It is easy to keep yourself busy with various tasks. But there are some things that should be taken care of before others. Then you can take time to relax and do fun things when the necessary things are already taken care of.

~ How do you prioritize your tasks?

38. "I take care of all my responsibilities."

We all have errands, projects, and chores that need to be taken care of in a timely way. Taking good care of yourself means carrying out your responsibilities.

~ What are your major responsibilities?

~ What are your minor responsibilities?

39. "I take on only the responsibilities that I can honestly handle."

Sometimes we do not want to miss out on something, we think that we can do more than we are able to, or we want to help another person. That is when we end up taking on more than we can handle. It is important not to over-commit yourself and cause unnecessary stress.

~ Do you ever over-extend yourself?

~ How do you feel when you over-extend yourself?

40. "I am able to finish what I started."

Sometimes we get excited about a project, but then we lose interest. Sometimes, once we get involved in a project, we begin to realize that it is taking more time and effort than we thought it would. And sometimes we take on several projects at a time, leaving no room for the completion of some things. Therefore, it is helpful to be aware of what is involved in a project.

~ Before beginning a project, do you take into account everything that it will involve?

~ How many projects have you started but have not yet completed?

~ In comparison, how often do you follow through with something until it is complete?

41. "I seek to be aware of the opportunities that come my way."
42. "I am open to discovering positive opportunities."

Opportunities appear in both minor and major ways. They are prospects for improvement or advancement. Favorable circumstances do not always present themselves in obvious ways. So you need to be on the lookout for them. And it is important to weed out the worthwhile opportunities from the ones that will not go in the direction that you want.

~ Are you attentive to the opportunities that present themselves to you?

~ Are you able to discern which opportunities are the best for you?

43. "I am conscious of the tools that I have available to me, and I use them in effective ways."

Tools can be skills as well as resources. We all have different talents and abilities. And we all have access to different resources.

~ What are your skills?

~ What resources are available to you?

~ How do you use your skills and resources?

44. "I am able to solve my problems in a reasonable way."

Throughout the course of life, we are always faced with various kinds of predicaments. Some problems are fairly easy to deal with. Some are not so easy. However, with groundedness and rational thinking, they can be taken care of in a reasonable way.

~ How do you handle the problems that come your way?

45. "I have the courage and patience to confront the problems that stand in my way."

No matter how stable and empowered we are, we are always going to be faced with some kinds of problems. It takes courage and patience to handle problems in a sensible manner.

~ Do you handle problems in a confident way?

~ Are you able to be patient while you work things through?

46. "I am able to face the challenges that confront me."
47. "I am able to learn from life's challenges."

Throughout our lives, we are continually faced with both minor and major challenges. They do not have to be blocks that stand in the way. Challenges should be viewed as opportunities to empower yourself.

~ How do you handle life's challenges?

48. "I take the time to understand the true nature of a situation before jumping to conclusions."

Sometimes it is easy to make assumptions about certain things before having all the facts about it. When you react to something before you know all the details, it can cause added complications. It is always best to wait until you know and understand what is really going on before drawing a conclusion.

~ Do you easily make assumptions about things, or do you think things through before coming to a conclusion?

49. "I take the time to make well-informed decisions."

There are times when a decision has to be made quickly. However, most decisions do not have to be made immediately. It is always helpful when you can take some time to think things through, and get the information that you need, before making a final decision. Well thought out choices tend to work out in a positive way.

~ Do you examine all aspects of a situation before making a decision?

50. "I educate myself, and I learn from my experiences."

Education is a key ingredient to empowerment. Knowledge helps you to achieve things. There are many ways to gain knowledge.

~ How do you educate yourself?

~ In what ways do you learn from your experiences?

51. "I learn from my mistakes."

Everyone makes mistakes. It is part of the human experience. The main thing is that we learn from our mistakes and that we do not make the same ones over and over again.

~ If something did not turn out the way that you wanted it to, how can you do it better next time?

52. "I am a student of life, and I am always learning."

Learning does not just happen from books or in a classroom setting. Our teachers are everywhere. Everyone and everything are our teachers. Learning never stops. It continues as long as we live.

~ Do you stay open-minded and receptive to new information?

53. "I listen to my inner wisdom."

Experience is a great teacher. Wisdom is the knowledge gained through experience. Wisdom is also connected with comprehension and insight. Listening to your inner wisdom is about slowing down and tuning in to your senses.

~ Do you use the knowledge and experience that you have gained?

~ Do you take time for quiet contemplation?

54. "I strive to be awake and aware."
55. "I strive for awareness and realization."

In today's stressful world it is easy to get caught up in the daily grind. We lose self-awareness, and become pre-occupied with mundane concerns. So we need to remind ourselves to regain consciousness and to stay conscious.

~ Is mindfulness a part of your regular routine?

56. "I strive for mental clarity."

Sometimes we need to clear away the mental clutter and distractions that keep us from focusing on what is most important. Think about the kinds of things that clutter your mind and make you feel distracted. Do not cling to these thoughts, but allow them to flow through you. Breathe deeply and let go.

~ How do you keep your mind clear?

57. "I am able to be honest with myself."

An integral part of being aware is being honest with yourself. Some people think that they know themselves very well. But many people really know very little about themselves. Being honest with yourself means facing everything you possibly can about who and what you are.

~ Are you truthful with yourself?

58. "I seek truth in all areas of my life."

In today's world, there exists a lot of false information and distortions. People fool themselves, and they fool each other. There are many reasons why this happens: control, entertainment, profit, and self-satisfaction. Recognizing the truth from the fictions helps to create positive energy.

~ How do you separate the facts from the falsehoods?

59. "I recognize that enlightenment is an ongoing process."

Enlightenment does not happen all at once. There are peak periods that one can experience, but enlightenment occurs over time through practice and education. And the path of enlightenment is not a straight line. It has its variations along the way.

~ What does enlightenment mean to you?

60. "I know when to step back and look at things in a different way."

Sometimes it is useful to view something in a different way. It is important not to get stuck in a rut. If something is not working out the way that you want it to, then it is time to refresh your perspective. When you take a step back, you can see things with another point of view.

~ Do you change your perspective from time to time?

61. "I am open to fresh ideas and new ways of doing things."

It is easy to get into certain habits and routines. Human beings are pretty much creatures of habit. We like what we know. Habit and routine can be a positive thing. However, it can sometimes get stale or outdated. So it is important to know when to look at something, or think about something, with a different perspective. This applies to minor as well as major things.
~ How do you feel about new and innovative ideas?

~ Are you able to take a fresh approach to something that has become outdated?

62. "I have the ability to be open-minded and consider various possibilities and options."
63. "I am aware of the choices and options that are available to me."

There are often more options available to us than we realize. Most situations have many facets. Take the time to think things through and do some research. Become aware of the possibilities.

~ Do you consider various options before you make a decision about something?

64. "I am a creative person."
65. "I enjoy being creative."

Everyone has the ability to be creative. There are many ways to be creative. Being creative means being imaginative and productive. You can bring that into any aspect of life.

~ How do you express your creativity?

66. "I use my imagination in positive and constructive ways."

Everyone has an imagination. If you dream while you sleep, you have an imagination. If you've ever told a story or a joke, you have an imagination. If you've ever drawn a picture, you have an imagination. If you watch movies or read books, you have an imagination. If you fantasize about winning the lottery, you have an imagination.

~ How do you use your imagination?

67. "I know when and where to seek inspiration."

To be inspired means to come up with ideas. There are many ways to find inspiration. If you are receptive to it, then it will happen for you.

~ Do you allow yourself to be open to inspiration?

~ How do you seek inspiration?

68. "I am aware of my intuitive senses."

Everyone has the capacity for intuition. It is natural to know things instinctually. You just have to tune in to your innate ability. Allow yourself to be aware of your senses.

~ How do you stay in tune with your intuition?

69. "I trust my instincts and gut feelings."

Your body is a very sensitive instrument. There was a time when human beings were much more attune to their bodies. Now we have to re-learn to develop this type of awareness.

~ Do you listen to what your body tells you?

~ Do you trust your instincts and follow your gut feelings?

70. "I am aware of my dreams and what they tell me."

Dreams are not just mental chatter. They tell us things about ourselves, other people, and the world around us. They are dramatic interpretations of the information that your mind absorbs. Your unconscious mind knows more than your conscious mind does, because it is not inhibited with anything.

~ Do you remember your dreams?

~ Do you pay attention to the messages that your dreams give you?

71. "I view life as an inspiring adventure."

We are multi-dimensional beings able to feel and interact with things on many levels. Your life is an exploration of your physical, mental, emotional, and spiritual characteristics and the discovery of how they work together. It should be a worthwhile experience.

~ What kind of an adventure are you having?

72. "I get satisfaction from the journey as much as I do from the end result."

Life is a journey through time. It is a path of discovery, a continuously dynamic and evolving voyage. There are twists and turns along the way. But the journey is meant to be savored and enjoyed.

~ How do you make your life a special journey for yourself?

73. "Every moment of my life is precious."
74. "Each moment is a new beginning."

Time is a constant flow of energy, a cycle of forward movement. It is empowering to be fully alive in the present without being hindered by the past.

~ Are you able to let go of the past?

~ Are you able to be fully alive in the moment?

75. "My time is a valuable resource."

Time is a one of the most precious commodities that we have. There is a limit to how long you will be in your physical body. Your time should be used wisely.

~ How often do you find yourself wishing that you had more time?

~ How often do you wish that your time had better quality?

~ How can you use your time wisely?

~ Where and how do you want to spend the time that you have?

76. "I am not controlled by impulse."

Sometimes it is fun or inspiring to do something on a whim. But when impulsiveness takes over and becomes an ongoing issue, this can be a problem. Being empowered means being able to manage yourself.

~ Do you have the ability to discipline yourself?

77. "I strive to overcome distractions."

There are lots of things that can distract us. Your attention can be diverted by many people and situations. Distractions can waste your time and energy.

~ How do you stay focused?

78. "I consider my options and take action at the appropriate time."
79. "I know when to take action."

Action is movement. It means taking charge of a situation. Action is putting a plan into practice. Positive action is knowing when to do something.

~ Are you able to put a plan into action when the time is right?

80. "I know when it is time to let go of something."

Oftentimes we continue to do something just because we are so much in the habit of doing it. Oftentimes we let things pile up, because we are hesitant to get rid of them or do not want to take the time to deal with them. Knowing when to let go helps to lighten your burdens.

~ Is there anything holding you back?

~ Are you able to let go when the time is right?

81. "I am open to positive change."
82. "I strive to be flexible and adaptable."

Change happens. And in today's world, change happens a lot. When there is change, old patterns transform and become new and different patterns. Positive change happens when you are able to go with the flow and make the best of what happens.

~ Are you able to go with the flow of life's ups and downs?

~ Do you allow positive changes to happen for you?

83. "I am the master of my own life."
84. "I am in control of my own life."
85. "I am not controlled by others."

There are many people and organizations that want to influence, manage, and rule us. And we often give our power away to them, either consciously or unconsciously. You are the person who has to live your life. Your personal power should be the greater influence in your own existence.

~ How do you maintain control over your own life?

86. "I am conscious of the behaviors of others and how they affect me."

The things that other people say and do have an affect on us. To some extent you create your own reality, but you are also dealing with everyone else's reality. The world is filled with different energies acting upon each other. You cannot control the thoughts and actions of others, but you can manage how you deal with other people.

~ Are you aware of how other people's words and actions affect you?

~ Do you deal with other people in a healthy and effective way?

87. "I know my worth."

It is healthy and empowering to experience a sense of value in this world. You should feel like you are getting and giving positive energy in your relationships. You should also be able to feel that you are contributing to society in a positive way.

~ What makes you feel worthwhile?

88. "I take responsibility for my own thoughts and actions."

You are the master of your own mind. It is easy to blame things on others such as your family and upbringing and the society that you live in. But ultimately, you are responsible for yourself.

~ Do you pay attention to your thoughts and behaviors?

~ Are you aware of how your actions affect others?

89. "I am able to communicate my thoughts, ideas, and feelings with clarity and confidence."

Communication is a vital part of life. It is important to speak clearly and specifically. People understand you better when you talk with clarity and confidence.

~ Are you aware of how you communicate to others?

~ If you realize that you have communicated in a way that another person does not understand, do you try to communicate in a way that the person does understand you?

90. "I am open to the support that others are able to give me."

Getting and giving support is an important part of creating stability in your life. Having a support system is part of your life's foundation. It is healthy to be able to connect with others and to allow others to connect with you.

~ Are you able to accept support from others?

91. "I give support to others when I am able to."

It is an essential part of life to be able to give support to others. There should always be a balance of give and take. A positive exchange of energies creates positive relationships.

~ Are you able to give support to others?

92. "I strive to be patient with myself and with others."

Tolerance is a key ingredient to healthy empowerment. And it is necessary for healthy relationships. When you treat others with patience, they will more likely respect you out of admiration rather than out of fear. When you are patient with others, they are more likely to be patient with you.

~ How do you show patience with your self?

~ How do you show patience with others?

93. "I am open to receiving positive energy."

Positive energy is uplifting. It helps to clear away negative energy. Too much negative energy is heavy and unhealthy. It is essential to well-being and empowerment to seek out sources of positive energy.

~ What do you do to clear away negative energy?

~ What do you do to bring in positive energy?

94. "I am filled with healthy energy, and I am surrounded with healthy energy."

Healthy energy creates health in all areas of your life. It is a life-affirming force. When people treat themselves and each other with respect and understanding, this is beneficial to existence.

~ How do you seek out healthy energy?

~ How do you create healthy energy?

95. "I work at transforming negative energy into positive energy."

Modern society has a tendency to generate negative energy. So it takes constant effort to shield yourself from it and to clear it from your own life. It is essential to establish healthy, positive energy for yourself.

~ How do you transform negative energy into positive energy?

96. "I conduct myself with integrity."

It is important to have respect for yourself. And it is equally important to have respect for other people and the world around you. Being accountable for your words and deeds creates positive energy.

~ How do you show respect for yourself and others?

97. "I know what my boundaries and limits are, and I maintain them."

Boundaries are where you end and someone else begins. Having clear boundaries with other people establishes health and empowerment. Limits are knowing how much you can deal with at any given time. Having solid limits also creates health and empowerment.

~ Are you attentive to your boundaries and limits?

98. "I know my limits and give only what I am capable of giving."

There are all kinds of people who want all kinds of things from us. Sometimes we are able to give, and sometimes we are not able to give. It is necessary to know with certainty when and how much to give or not give.

~ Do you know when you are able to give and how much to give?

99. "I am comfortable saying no when I really need to, and I am able to stick with my decision."

Having strong boundaries and limits often requires saying no to someone. When you say no, you have to be unyielding and uncompromising. If you are certain in your decisions, others will respect you.

~ Are you able to say no when you really want to, and are you able to uphold your decision?

100. "I am able to stand my ground when I need to."

Sometimes when you say no to someone, they continue to haggle with you. That is when it is time to stand your ground and embody your personal power.

~ Are you able to be firm with others when you are challenged?

101. "I am comfortable with my individuality."

It is healthy to have a strong sense of personal identity. It is empowering to know who you are apart from others. When you are empowered as an individual, you take an active role in the direction of your life.

~ Are you comfortable with your separateness from others?

~ Do you allow your personality to flourish?

~ What do you like most about yourself?

102. "I follow the path that I choose."
103. "I follow the path that is right for me."

Sometimes it is necessary to go along with others. But there are also times when it is necessary to follow your own way. Cooperation is important, but following your spirit is also important. If you balance your physical, mental, emotional, and spiritual desires, you will find your direction.

~ What is the path that is right for you?

104. "I am able to flow with the ups and downs of life."
105. "I am in tune with the flow of life's cycles."
106. "I acknowledge and honor the transitions that I make."

Life is filled with movement and cycles. There is always a current of minor and major changes. It is empowering to acknowledge where you have been, where you are, and where you are going.

~ Are you aware of the changes that take place in your life?

~ Do you acknowledge the transitions that occur?

~ In what ways do you honor the transitions that occur?

107. "I plant seeds, cultivate them, and watch them grow."

A seed is a possibility, a beginning, a prospect. When you plant a seed, you have started something new. If you want the seed to grow, you have to cultivate it.

~ In the garden of life, what do you bring to fruition?

108. "I do my best to live in balance."

You are a system within a system. There is a connection between you and the rest of the world. Living in balance does not mean that there is a constant state of equilibrium. The scales will always fluctuate a bit from side to side. The task is to keep them at a manageable state.

~ What does living in balance mean to you?

109. "I take time to nourish my soul."

Your soul is a multi-faceted jewel that needs to be honored. It is the essence of your being that brings you to life and gives you consciousness. There are many ways to feed your soul.

~ How do you nourish your soul?

110. "I give thanks for the blessings in my life."

Appreciation is an integral part of a balanced and healthy life. When you express gratitude, you are reminding yourself of what you have. When you are aware of what is good in your life, you will not take it for granted. Gratitude is also a way of putting focus on positive energy.

~ Do you take the time to appreciate what you have?

~ What are you thankful for?

~ In what ways do you show thanks?

~ Money Power ~

1. "I understand the power of money."

In our society, money is a source of empowerment. To begin with, it provides for all of our basic needs such as food, clothing, and shelter. Money is a tool that people use for many reasons. It can be used for constructive or destructive purposes.

~ Do you appreciate the power of money?

~ How do you use your money constructively?

2. "I have a positive relationship with money."

All around us, there are all kinds of ideas, attitudes, and feelings about money. This all has an affect on your psyche. And your conscious and unconscious beliefs affect your relationship with money.

~ What are your true thoughts and feelings about money?

~ What are the messages about money that you learned in the family that you grew up with?

~ What are the beliefs that hold you back?

~ What are the beliefs that impel you forward?

3. "I envision abundance in my life."

In order to have abundance, you need to be able to visualize it. You have to believe in the possibility of abundance. You also need to be patient in the time it takes to build your assets.

~ How do you envision abundance in your life?

~ What does abundance mean to you?

4. "I embrace prosperity in my life."
5. "I know how to attract prosperity and abundance."
6. "I am open to positive prosperity and abundance."
7. "My life is blessed with abundance."

    Abundance and prosperity in our lives gives us stability and groundedness. When our needs are being taken care of, we have a sense of safety and comfort. It is easier to enjoy life when all of the bills are paid and there is plenty of food to eat. Abundance is a state that happens in many different ways. It also appears in other forms besides money.

~ Do you feel comfortable with prosperity?

~ In what areas of your life do you feel prosperous?

~ How do you attract prosperity?

8. "My money is a valuable resource."

    Most of us work hard for the money that we earn. We put in many hours at a job in order to receive pay. Remember that your time is valuable, and your money is valuable.

~ Do you view your money as a source of worth?

9. "I manage my money in a practical way."

Having prosperity and abundance requires good money management. It is necessary to regularly balance your budget. Get into the habit of frequently assessing your income, what your financial needs are, and what current costs are.

~ Do you handle your income in a practical way?

10. "My financial goals are an important part of my life."

In order to have financial success, it is necessary to have clear goals concerning your money. If you are certain about what you want to do with your money, you will likely use it in a sensible way rather than squandering it.

~ What are your financial goals?

~ What are the reasons for each of your financial goals?

11. "I learn about and understand financial investing."

It is important to have money put away for the future, in case of unemployment or illness. In addition, it is necessary to save for retirement. Investments also allow you to have money for vacations, a new car, or other major expenditures. Before investing your money in anything, it is a good idea to learn about and understand the various ways to invest money.

~ Do you know about and understand the various ways to invest money?

12. "I do research before I make a large investment."

	Any kind of investment is usually a risk, although some are riskier than others. Begin by investing in low risk ventures. It is wise to invest in high risk undertakings only when you have the extra resources to do so. There are numerous books, magazines, and newsletters available that can teach you about financial investing.

~ Do you take the time to study the available resources on financial investing?

13. "I know how to utilize good financial strategies."

	Financial well-being involves skillful planning. Begin by investing in stable ventures. Invest in more risky ventures only when you have the extra income. And remember to keep track of your investments and how they are doing. If a particular investment is not doing well, it is time to reconsider that venture.

~ What is your financial plan?

14. "I pay attention to and stay knowledgeable about current trends."

	There are many factors that impact the economy and the social system. These factors can happen on the local level as well as the global level. The media also has a large influence on economic and social trends. Pay attention to interest rates and the rising cost of different commodities and services.

~ How do you keep informed about current trends that affect the economy and social system?

15. "I invest my money wisely."

You invest your money because you want it to be there in the future. You also want it to have grown and increased in value. That is why it is important to invest it wisely.

~ Do you exercise care in how you use your money?

16. "My financial investments are diverse."

One of the most essential rules of financial investing is to have a diverse portfolio. If you focus on one area, or devote everything to one thing, you will have lost a lot of time and/or money if it falters. Of course, you do not want to spread your money around too much, either. This is because too many investments can be difficult to keep track of.

~ Do you vary your financial investments?

17. "My investments bring me abundance and prosperity."

If you work progressively toward your goals, stay within your budget, and invest wisely and diversely you should experience abundance and prosperity.

~ How does wealth manifest for you?

18. "I have many assets and resources."

Assets and resources come in many forms. They can be financial, they can be material, and they can be mental or physical. You can invest in education, clothing for a job, or equipment for a business.

~ What are your assets and resources?

19. "I build and maintain financial stability in my life."
20. "Financial security is a priority for me."

It is important to have monetary stability and security. Then you will be covered in case of illness, unemployment, or any other problem. You will also have finances for your older years, whether you retire or not.

~ How you do create financial stability and security for yourself?

21. "I know how to provide for all of my needs."
22. "All of my needs are taken care of."

　　It is essential to believe in plenty rather than scarcity. Be resourceful, and do not let the economic and political climate have too much of an impact on your emotions.

~ Are you able to take care of your needs in order of priority?

23. "I live well within my means."

　　To live within your means is to spend within the parameters of what you earn. To live beyond your means is to get yourself into debt. It is always best to avoid getting into debt, especially credit card debt. To live comfortably, you do not have to "keep up with the Jones's."

~ How do you live well within your means?

24. "I spend my money carefully."
25. "I am careful with my spending habits."
26. "I buy only what I can afford."

Remember to have strong boundaries and limits when it comes to spending your money. Today, there are vastly more commodities and services available than ever before. And there is an abundance of advertising to go along with these things. We are constantly tempted by merchants selling their wares. We are often told that we need things that we do not really need. It is necessary to consider this, and stay within your budget.

~ Do you spend within your budget?

27. "I keep track of my expenditures."

All those dollars spent add up. Money can go quickly if you do not watch how you are using it. It is also very important to pay attention to your bills and bank statements. Sometimes companies charge fees for services that we do not need or want. In these days of plastic cards and electronic payments it can be easy to lose track of expenditures. So it is necessary to stay aware of your transactions.

~ Do you know where your money goes?

28. "I pay all of my bills on time, and I keep accurate records of my payments."

When you pay your bills on time, you do not have to pay late fees or receive reminders to pay what you owe. If you keep accurate records, then any dispute with a company can be challenged and corrected. It is also important to maintain documentation for tax purposes.

~ Do you pay your bills on or before the due date?

~ Do you maintain accurate documentation of the bills that you paid?

29. "I am generous without being frivolous."

Generosity can be a positive thing. It is important to acknowledge and help others. But it can be detrimental when your generosity is squandered.

~ Are you able to give without giving too much?

30. "I take care of the things that I own."

We spend money on cars, appliances, household items, clothing, computers, stereos, televisions, and various other objects. Material things represent your time and work. Cleaning and maintaining your possessions helps them to last longer.

~ Do you clean and maintain your possessions?

31. "I am organized and clutter free."

Being organized and clutter free helps to save time and money. When you know where everything is, an item can be found quickly. When you have ready access to an item, you do not have to buy an extra one because you are unable to find the one that you already have. Putting things in order is not a difficult task. All it takes is some effort.

~ How do you make physical and mental space for yourself?

32. "I get rid of the things that I no longer need or want."

If you do not need or want an item anymore, then do away with it. Do not let it take up space in a corner, closet, or garage. Sell it, give it away, or throw it away.

~ Do you know when it is time to get rid of something?

33. "My career is an important part of my life."

Work is usually something that you spend a lot of time at. So it should be something that you really want to be doing. Sometimes the work we do for money is different from the work we do for ambition. It can take time to build a successful career.

~ Is your work an important part of your life?

34. "I am pursuing the career of my choice."

Working at a career that you choose to work at can be very fulfilling. When you do what you enjoy, you have pride in your efforts. You feel like you are doing something meaningful.

~ Are you pursuing the vocation that you want to?

35. "I enjoy great success in my career."

Achieving success does not often happen quickly. It usually requires a consistent effort toward progress. If you really want something, be persistent. Determination pays off.

~ How can you or do you achieve success in your career?

36. "I am building a strong foundation for myself."

Financial and vocational stability creates a strong ground for you. It puts you in an advantageous position. When you have a strong foundation, you are not easily ungrounded. In case of a setback, you can usually recover fairly quickly. You can also continue to build on what you already have.

~ In what ways do you create a strong foundation for yourself?

37. "I enjoy both inner and outer wealth."

Establishing stability means creating a balance. In the pursuit of the almighty dollar, it is important to take care of your heart and soul. There is a lot more to life than money and material goods.

~ How do you create a balance between your inner and outer riches?

~ Love Power ~

1. "My emotions are grounded and balanced."

　　Emotions are part of what makes us human. It is normal and natural to feel a full spectrum of emotions. In order to experience emotions in a healthy way, it is important to balance them. Otherwise, you can become swept away by your feelings.

~ How do you balance your emotions?

~ What gives you emotional stability?

~ How do you channel your feelings?

2. "I am able to accept and integrate my feelings and emotions."

We react to different situations in different ways. The key to dealing with feelings and emotions is to understand what you are feeling and why you are feeling that way. Then you can absorb and regulate your emotions and not be ruled by them.

~ Are you able to recognize all of your feelings and emotions?

~ How do you handle your feelings and emotions?

3. "I express my feelings in healthy ways."

　　Emotional expression is necessary for wholeness and well-being. It is not healthy to suppress your feelings. It is also unhealthy to allow your emotions to be expressed uncontrollably.

~ How do you express your feelings in a balanced way?

4. "I am able to feel passion without being overwhelmed by it."

Passion is a wonderful feeling as long as it is expressed with balance. It is important not to let it turn into an addiction. Passion can be invigorating when channeled in a healthy way.

~ How do you manage your passion?

5. "I am able to experience desire without feeling obsessed."

Desire is a creative feeling. It is the spark that ignites activity and forward movement. But when the desire overtakes you and becomes a fixation, this can be a problem. Being too needy can push someone away. And focusing too much on one thing can take time and energy away from other things.

~ What does the feeling of desire mean to you?

~ How do you express your desire?

6. "I am balanced within myself and with the world around me."

We are all part of the world that we live in. We have different kinds of relationships with different kinds of people. Positive relationships are achieved by developing positive energy. Creating a balance within yourself helps to create a balance outside of yourself.

~ How do you generate inner and outer balance?

7. "I am attractive and lovable."

In order to be attractive, it is necessary to feel attractive. There are many ways to look and feel attractive. Being attractive does not mean being "Hollywood" gorgeous. Attractiveness is an energy that you exude.

~ What makes you feel attractive?

~ How do you make yourself attractive to others?

8. "I give myself love, and I allow myself to be loved."

Loving yourself means taking care of yourself. It also means giving yourself patience and acceptance. When you give yourself love, you are more able to accept love from others.

~ How do you give yourself love?

~ How do you allow yourself to be loved?

9. "My heart is nourished with love."
10. "Love is a positive force in my life."

Love exists in many forms. It is a feeling of caring and acceptance. Love is about being receptive to yourself, others, and the world around you.

~ How do you nourish your heart with love?

~ How do you invite love into your life?

11. "Love is a journey of discovery and growth."

Love is a feeling of connectedness. It opens the heart. And when the heart opens, it creates a sensitivity to your feelings and emotions. It also creates a sensitivity to who and what is around you. This opening and awareness creates an opportunity for discovery and growth.

~ Are you receptive to what love reveals to you?

12. "I am aware of what I need and want in order to have a fulfilling relationship."

In order to find a relationship that can work for you, you need to know what is important to you in a relationship. You need to find someone who you are compatible with. The more that the two of you have in common, the more likely that it will be successful.

~ What are you looking for in a relationship?

13. "I know what attributes I want in a romantic partner."

A lasting relationship requires knowing what you want and need in a partner. Think about the long term. Your partner is someone who you will be spending a lot of time with. Do not choose someone out of desperation. When you come from a place of strength, rather than weakness, you will be more likely to get what you want.

~ What qualities do you want and need in a partner?

14. "I am attracting a partner who is right for me."

Attracting a partner requires that you be open to the likelihood of this happening. In order to attract the right partner, you need to be in the right places. You need to make yourself available to someone who you can make a positive connection with.

~ How do you increase the likelihood that you will meet someone who is right for you?

15. "I am able to maintain my individuality while being in a romantic relationship with someone."

Interdependence is a positive thing. A couple should be able to share and cooperate. But it is important not to become enmeshed in a relationship and lose your sense of self.

~ How do you maintain your sense of self in a relationship?

16. "I am able to make a commitment in a relationship."

The most necessary ingredient to a healthy and lasting relationship is the ability to make a commitment. Making a commitment means dealing with all the issues of being in a relationship. When you make a commitment, you share in a partnership.

~ How do you feel about commitment in a relationship?

17. "I strive to have reasonable expectations in romantic love."

We are exposed to a lot of stories, ideas, and images about romantic love. Most of it is fantasy. It is important to have a sensible perspective of romantic love. When you are realistic, your relationship has a better chance of working out.

~ What ideas and images about romantic love did you grow up with?

~ What are your past experiences with romantic love?

~ What is your perspective on romantic love?

18. "I seek and maintain healthy relationships with other people."
19. "I spend time engaged in enjoyable activities with other people."

We are all social beings, and positive social contact is essential for emotional well-being. We need to have healthy relationships with family members, friends, and acquaintances. A vital ingredient of a positive relationship is the ability to connect with others in addition to your partner.

~ Do you make the time for social activities?

~ How do you connect with other people?

20. "I enjoy socializing with positive people."

Health and wholeness are enhanced by spending time with positive people. The positive energy that they exude is uplifting and invigorating.

~ Who are the positive people in your life?

21. "I treat others with consideration."
22. "I am thoughtful and compassionate."

It is important to respect other people and the world around you. Everyone and everything is inter-connected. We all affect each other in different ways. When you are considerate of others, you are also being considerate of yourself.

~ How do you show concern for others?
~ In what ways do you show thoughtfulness and compassion?

23. "I am able to make compromises when it is reasonable to do so."

In order to get along well with others, it is necessary to be cooperative. Sometimes you get what you want. Sometimes the other person gets what he or she wants. And sometimes you both get a reasonable compromise.

~ How do you show cooperation with others?

24. "I seek stability in my relationships."

Stability is a necessary ingredient in a healthy relationship. Being psychologically available to the people who you care about, and knowing that someone is available to you, creates a positive flow of energy.

~ Are you able to create stability in your relationships with other people?

25. "I accept and love my partner for the person who he or she is."

A successful relationship requires valuing the wholeness of the person who you are romantically involved with. It is essential to love the person for who they are, not what you want them to be.

~ Are you involved with or seeking a companion who you feel comfortable with?

26. "I communicate well with my partner."

A healthy relationship requires good communication. It is necessary to discuss issues and share thoughts, feelings, and ideas. And it is essential to talk about certain subjects at the right time.

~ Are you able to communicate your thoughts and feelings in a healthy way?

~ Do you discuss relationship issues with your partner at appropriate times?

27. "I am able to listen attentively to another person."

Part of being able to communicate well is being able to listen. That means being fully present with the other person, and actually hearing what that other person is saying.

~ Are you attentive to what other people say?

~ Do you make an effort to understand what another person says?

28. "I am aware of how my behavior affects others."
29. "I respect the boundaries and limits of other people."

Your words and actions have an effect on other people. Your behaviors also influence how others respond to you. Positive energy is created when you are aware of how you handle yourself around others. And through your words and actions, it is important to show consideration for the boundaries of others.

~ Do you pay attention to your words and actions?

~ Are you aware of, and show respect for, other people's limits?

30. "I am able to accept affection and show affection."

Part of being able to connect with another person is the ability to show warmth. Affection is not just about physical contact, it is also about mental and emotional connection.

~ Are you an affectionate person?

31. "I am comfortable with physical and emotional intimacy with my partner."

A successful romantic relationship requires a healthy sense of closeness. The extent of the physical and emotional intimacy depends on the stage of the relationship. It is essential to move at an appropriate pace.

~ How do you feel about physical and emotional intimacy?

32. "I am comfortable with my sexuality."
33. "I express my sexuality in healthy and positive ways."

Sexuality is a normal, natural part of being human. It is also a normal part of a healthy romantic relationship. Therefore, it is important to be comfortable with sensuality, physical attraction, and intimacy. Healthy sexuality is a celebration of life and an expression of sacred union.

~ What are the messages about sexuality that you received while you were growing up?

~ What are the messages about sexuality that are currently around you?

~ What are your thoughts and feelings about sexuality?

~ How do you express your sexuality?

34. "I enjoy being romantic with my partner."

Romance adds to the enjoyment of a relationship. There are many ways to be romantic. When you continue to woo one another throughout the course of time, you keep the excitement alive.

~ What does romance mean to you?

~ How do you keep the romance alive in your relationship?

35. "I invite happiness into my life."

    Being happy means being satisfied with yourself and with your life. Happiness is not a constant state of bliss. It is about acceptance and allowing yourself to enjoy the connections that you make on a daily basis.

~ What makes you feel happy?

~ How do you create happiness for yourself?

~ How do you interact with life?

Appendix

~ Personal Power ~

1. "I am grounded and connected in my body." ~ Page 4
2. "I am grounded and connected with the earth." ~ 4
3. "I am fully present in my body." ~ 5
4. "I am fully present in the world." ~ 5
5. "My body is sacred." ~ 5
6. "I feel comfortable in my body." ~ 6
7. "I take care of my body and my health." ~ 6
8. "I take good care of myself, and I know how to heal myself." ~ 6
9. "I am able to heal myself when I am feeling stressed and tense." ~ 7
10. "I exercise regularly and keep myself physically fit." ~ 7
11. "I consistently replenish myself." ~ 7
12. "I am nourished by the powers Nature." ~ 8
13. "I remember to breathe fully and deeply." ~ 8
14. "I get plenty of clean, fresh air." ~ 8
15. "I expose myself to a healthy amount of light." ~ 9
16. "I regularly replenish my body with fresh, clean water." ~ 9
17. "I have a positive and healthy relationship with food." ~ 9
18. "I take the time to learn about proper diet and nutrition." ~ 10
19. "I use my energy in healthy and balanced ways." ~ 10
20. "I create stability within myself and in my environment. ~ 11
21. "I am stable and well grounded." ~ 11
22. "I give myself support and comfort." ~ 11
23. "I give myself time for relaxation and recreation." ~ 11
24. "I am able to relax and let go." ~ 12
25. "I take care of my emotional well-being." ~ 12
26. "I know how to ask for assistance from others." ~ 12
27. "I have a healthy sense of humor." ~ 13
28. "My home is a safe and comfortable place." ~ 13
29. "I am centered in my body, mind, emotions, and spirit." ~ 13
30. "I work to maintain a balance between my spiritual needs and my material needs." ~ 14
31. "I have a healthy sense of self confidence." ~ 14
32. "I seek to empower myself in healthy and balanced ways." ~ 14
33. "I have realistic goals for my future." ~ 15

34. "I am accomplishing my goals with great success." ~ 15
35. "I am comfortable with success." ~ 16
36. "I am able to make practical decisions." ~ 16
37. "I know what my priorities are, and I take care of them first." ~ 16
38. "I take care of all my responsibilities." ~ 16
39. "I take on only the responsibilities that I can honestly handle." ~ 17
40. "I am able to finish what I started." ~ 17
41. "I seek to be aware of the opportunities that come my way." ~ 18
42. "I am open to discovering positive opportunities." ~ 18
43. "I am conscious of the tools that I have available to me, and I use them in effective ways." ~ 18
44. "I am able to solve my problems in a reasonable way." ~ 18
45. "I have the courage and patience to confront the problems that stand in my way." ~ 19
46. "I am able to face the challenges that confront me." ~ 19
47. "I am able to learn from life's challenges." ~ 19
48. "I take the time to understand the true nature of a situation before jumping to conclusions." ~ 19
49. "I take the time to make well-informed decisions." ~ 20
50. "I educate myself and I learn from my experiences." ~ 20
51. "I learn from my mistakes." ~ 20
52. "I am a student of life, and I am always learning." ~ 21
53. "I listen to my inner wisdom." ~ 21
54. "I strive to be awake and aware." ~ 21
55. "I strive for awareness and realization." ~ 21
56. "I strive for mental clarity." ~ 22
57. "I am able to be honest with myself." ~ 22
58. "I seek truth in all areas of my life." ~ 22
59. "I recognize that enlightenment is an ongoing process." ~ 23
60. "I know when to step back and look at things in a different way." ~ 23
61. "I am open to fresh ideas and new ways of doing things." ~ 23
62. "I have the ability to be open-minded and consider various possibilities and options." ~ 24
63. "I am aware of the choices and options that are available to me." ~ 24
64. "I am a creative person." ~ 24
65. "I enjoy being creative." ~ 24
66. "I use my imagination in positive and constructive ways." ~ 24
67. "I know when and where to seek inspiration." ~ 24
68. "I am aware of my intuitive senses." ~ 25
69. "I trust my instincts and gut feelings." ~ 25

70. "I am aware of my dreams and what they tell me." ~ 25
71. "I view life as an inspiring adventure." ~ 26
72. "I get satisfaction from the journey as much as I do from the end result." ~ 26
73. "Every moment of my life is precious." ~ 26
74. "Each moment is a new beginning." ~ 26
75. "My time is a valuable resource." ~ 27
76. "I am not controlled by impulse." ~ 27
77. "I strive to overcome distractions." ~ 27
78. "I consider my options and take action at the appropriate time." ~ 28
79. "I know when to take action." ~ 28
80. "I know when it is time to let go of something." ~ 28
81. "I am open to positive change." ~ 28
82. "I strive to be flexible and adaptable." ~ 28
83. "I am the master of my own life." ~ 29
84. "I am in control of my own life." ~ 29
85. "I am not controlled by others." ~ 29
86. "I am conscious of the behaviors of others and how they affect me." ~ 29
87. "I know my worth." ~ 29
88. "I take responsibility for my own thoughts and actions." ~ 30
89. "I am able to communicate my thoughts, ideas, and feelings with clarity and confidence." ~ 30
90. "I am open to the support that others are able to give me." ~ 30
91. "I give support to others when I am able to." ~ 31
92. "I strive to be patient with myself and with others." ~ 31
93. "I am open to receiving positive energy." ~ 31
94. "I am filled with healthy energy, and I am surrounded with healthy energy." ~ 32
95. "I work at transforming negative energy into positive energy." ~ 32
96. "I conduct myself with integrity." ~ 32
97. "I know what my boundaries and limits are, and I maintain them." ~ 33
98. "I know my limits and give only what I am capable of giving." ~ 33
99. "I am comfortable saying no when I really need to, and I am able to stick with my decision." ~ 33
100. "I am able to stand my ground when I need to." ~ 34
101. "I am comfortable with my individuality." ~ 34
102. "I follow the path that I choose." ~ 34
103. "I follow the path that is right for me." ~ 34
104. "I am able to flow with the ups and downs of life." ~ 35
105. "I am in tune with the flow of life's cycles." ~ 35

106. "I acknowledge and honor the transitions that I make." ~ 35
107. "I plant seeds, cultivate them, and watch them grow." ~ 35
108. "I do my best to live in balance." ~ 35
109. "I take time to nourish my soul." ~ 36
110. "I give thanks for the blessings in my life." ~ 36

~ Money Power ~

1. "I understand the power of money." ~ Page 37
2. "I have a positive relationship with money." ~ 37
3. "I envision abundance in my life." ~ 38
4. "I embrace prosperity in my life." ~ 38
5. "I know how to attract prosperity and abundance." ~ 38
6. "I am open to positive prosperity and abundance." ~ 38
7. "My life is blessed with abundance." ~ 38
8. "My money is a valuable resource." ~ 38
9. "I manage my money in a practical way." ~ 39
10. "My financial goals are an important part of my life." ~ 39
11. "I learn about and understand financial investing." ~ 39
12. "I do research before I make a large investment." ~ 40
13. "I know how to utilize good financial strategies." ~ 40
14. "I pay attention to and stay knowledgeable about current trends." ~ 40
15. "I invest my money wisely." ~ 41
16. "My financial investments are diverse." ~ 41
17. "My investments bring me abundance and prosperity." ~ 41
18. "I have many assets and resources." ~ 41
19. "I build and maintain financial stability in my life." ~ 42
20. "Financial security is a priority for me." ~ 42
21. "I know how to provide for all of my needs." ~ 42
22. "All of my needs are taken care of." ~ 42
23. "I live well within my means." ~ 42
24. "I spend my money carefully." ~ 43
25. "I am careful with my spending habits." ~ 43
26. "I buy only what I can afford." ~ 43
27. "I keep track of my expenditures." ~ 43
28. "I pay all my bills on time, and I keep accurate records of my payments." ~ 43
29. "I am generous without being frivolous." ~ 44

30. "I take care of the things that I own." ~ 44
31. "I am organized and clutter free." ~ 44
32. "I get rid of the things that I no longer need or want." ~ 44
33. "My career is an important part of my life." ~ 45
34. "I am pursuing the career of my choice." ~ 45
35. "I enjoy great success in my career." ~ 45
36. "I am building a strong foundation for myself." ~ 45
37. "I enjoy both inner and outer wealth." ~ 46

~ Love Power ~

1. "My emotions are grounded and balanced." ~ Page 47
2. "I am able to accept and integrate my feelings and emotions." ~ 47
3. "I express my feelings in healthy ways." ~ 47
4. "I am able to feel passion without being overwhelmed by it." ~ 48
5. "I am able to experience desire without feeling obsessed." ~ 48
6. "I am balanced within myself and with the world around me." ~ 48
7. "I am attractive and lovable." ~ 49
8. "I give myself love, and I allow myself to be loved." ~ 49
9. "My heart is nourished with love." ~ 49
10. "Love is a positive force in my life." ~ 49
11. "Love is a journey of growth and discovery." ~ 50
12. "I am aware of what I need and want in order to have a fulfilling relationship." ~ 50
13. "I know what attributes I want in a romantic partner." ~ 50
14. "I am attracting a partner who is right for me." ~ 51
15. "I am able to maintain my individuality while being in a romantic relationship with someone." ~ 51
16. "I am able to make a commitment in a relationship." ~ 51
17. "I strive to have reasonable expectations in romantic love." ~ 52
18. "I seek and maintain healthy relationships with other people." ~ 52
19. "I spend time engaged in enjoyable activities with other people." ~ 52
20. "I enjoy socializing with positive people." ~ 52
21. "I treat others with consideration." ~ 53
22. "I am thoughtful and compassionate." ~ 53
23. "I am able to make compromises when it is reasonable to do so." ~ 53
24. "I seek stability in my relationships." ~ 53
25. "I accept my partner for the person that she or he is." ~ 54

26. "I communicate well with my partner." ~ 54
27. "I am able to listen attentively to another person." ~ 54
28. "I am aware of how my behavior affects others." ~ 55
29. "I respect the boundaries and limits of other people." ~ 55
30. "I am able to accept affection and show affection." ~ 55
31. "I am comfortable with physical and emotional intimacy." ~ 55
32. "I am comfortable with my sexuality." ~ 56
33. "I express my sexuality in healthy and positive ways." ~ 56
34. "I enjoy being romantic with my partner." ~ 56
35. "I invite happiness into my life." ~ 57

About the Author

Conny Jasper has a Master's Degree in Counseling Psychology. She has worked as a counselor, consultant, and teacher for over thirty years. Conny is an artist, a poet, and an accomplished writer. She is also a certified Reiki Master and a certified yoga instructor. For more advanced learning in personal growth and empowerment, you may contact Conny for individual sessions.

www.ingramcontent.com/pod-product-compliance
Lightning Source LLC
LaVergne TN
LVHW061316060426
835507LV00019B/2181

9780988936102